FRACTURED
fairytales

The stories of Humpty Dumpty, Little Miss Muffet and a host of other well-known nursery rhyme and fairytale characters all get retold in this hilarious new collection compiled by Ann Weld. Have you ever wondered why Robin Hood stole from the rich and not from the poor, or considered what would happen if Little Red Riding Hood's grandma turned the tables on the big bad wolf? The answers are inside this book along with an electrifying new tale of the three little pigs and a rather alarming rendition of the tale of Sleeping Beauty. Max Fatchen, Bill Scott, Robin Klein, Colin Thiele, Dianne Bates and Barbara Giles are just a few of the poets who had fun putting this collection together. And when you've read it you'll know why! A great book for younger readers.

FRACTURED
fairytales
&
Ruptured
Rhymes

Compiled by
Ann Weld

Illustrated by
Craig Smith

AN OMNIBUS/PUFFIN BOOK

Omnibus Books
52 Fullarton Road
Norwood, South Australia 5067

Penguin Books Australia Ltd,
487 Maroondah Highway, PO Box 257,
Ringwood, Victoria 3134, Australia
Penguin Books Ltd,
Harmondsworth, Middlesex, England
Penguin Books,
40 West 23rd Street, New York, NY 10010 USA
Penguin Books Canada Limited,
2801 John Street, Markham, Ontario, Canada L3R 1B4
Penguin Books (NZ) Ltd,
182–190 Wairau Road, Auckland 10, New Zealand

First published by Omnibus Books in association
with Penguin Books Australia Ltd 1990
Poems copyright © individual authors 1990
This selection copyright © Omnibus Books 1990
Illustrations copyright © Craig Smith 1990

Typeset in Australia by Caxtons Pty Ltd, Adelaide
Made and printed in Australia by The Book Printer,
Maryborough, Victoria

CIP

Fractured fairytales and ruptured rhymes.

Includes index.
ISBN 0 14 034402 0.

1. Children's poetry, Australian. I. Weld, Ann. II.
Smith, Craig, 1955–

A821.30809282

Contents

Funny Money

Simple Simon met a pieman
Going to the fair.
Said Simple Simon to the pieman,
"Let me taste your ware."
Said the pieman to Simple Simon,
"Show me first your penny."
Said Simple Simon to the pieman,
"Indeed, I have not any.
Pennies went out years ago,
Stop trying to be funny.
Just charge it to my credit card—
I've only plastic money.

Michael Dugan

Road Alert

Simple Simon
Hit a pieman
On the motorway.
Neither chap was badly hurt.
The pieman tore his favourite shirt,
But Simon's hair,
So neat and wavy,
Reeked for weeks of meat and gravy.

Redmond Phillips

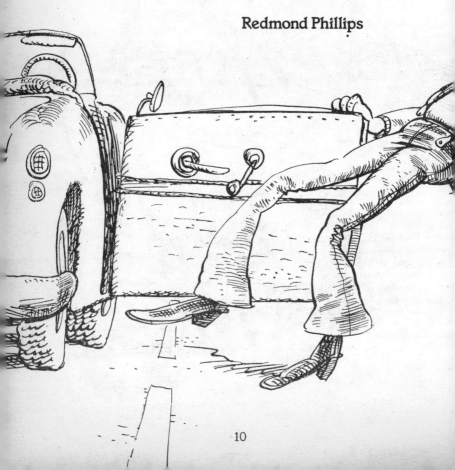

Not So Simple

Simple Simon wasn't simple.
He was ultra cool—
Just pretending to be simple
So he'd miss out school.

Allyson Lane

Sing a Song of Chaos

Sing a song of sixpence,
A pocketful of rye,
Four-and-twenty cockies
Baked in a pie.
When the pie was opened
The birds began to squawk,
And nobody for miles around
Could hear themselves talk.

Dan Vallely

Sing a Song of Six Cents

Sing a song of six cents
And lots and lots of rye,
Humpty Dumpty's underpants
Are flying through the sky.
Along came the blackbirds
And carried them away.
How he got them back again
I really cannot say.

Joy Sidey and Angela Sidey

Egged On

Humpty Dumpty sat on the wall,
Humpty Dumpty had a great fall.
Surely they knew that in such a place
Humpty would finish with egg on
    his face.

Colin Thiele

Rotten!

Humpty Dumpty sat in his bed,
Bandages wrapped around his head.
He moaned, "Of all the rotten tricks!
Who's the one that greased the bricks?"

Craig Christie

Darting Around

The Queen of Hearts
She threw some darts
Over the garden wall.
The Knave of Hearts
He stopped those darts
And no one heard him fall.

Janeen Brian

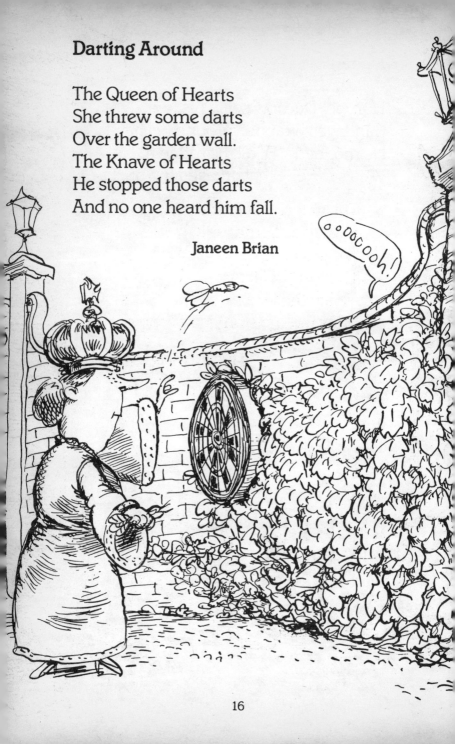

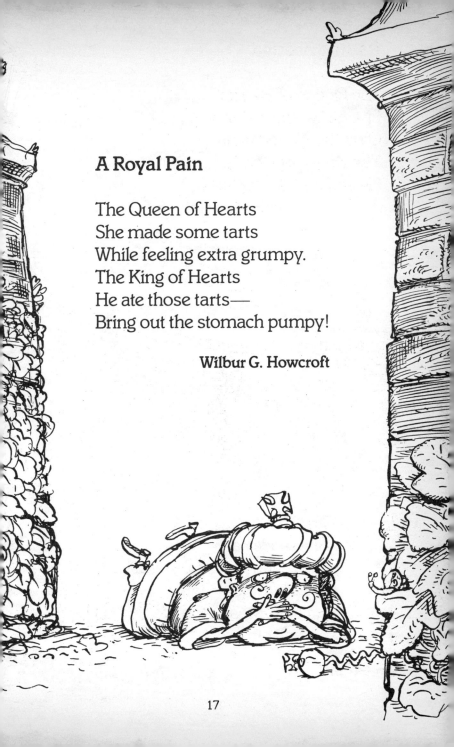

A Royal Pain

The Queen of Hearts
She made some tarts
While feeling extra grumpy.
The King of Hearts
He ate those tarts—
Bring out the stomach pumpy!

Wilbur G. Howcroft

Sick at Heart

The Queen of Hearts
She made some tarts
With cabbage, beans and lard.
The Knave of Hearts
He stole those tarts . . .
Serves him right.

Craig Christie

Tart Attack

The Queen of Hearts
She made some tarts
All on a summer's day;
The Knave of Hearts
He stole those tarts,
And with them ran away.

The Queen of Hearts
Wouldn't make any more tarts.
"What's the use?" she said.
"They're always getting nicked."

Dianne Bates

Robbin' Hood

Now Robin Hood, of ancient lore,
Took from the rich but not the poor,
And so goes down in tale and song
As one quite innocent of wrong.
But if one cares to think it through
One sees another point of view.
His so-called goodness was a fake—
The poor had nought for him to take.

Wilbur G. Howcroft

Sold Short

She sells sea shells by the sea shore;
She sells sea shells to tourists by
    the score.
(If those gullible tourists just looked they
    would see
Thousands of shells they could pick up
    for free!)

Robin Klein

Out of Line

There was a crooked man
Who ran a crooked mile.
He wore a crooked prison suit
And had a crooked smile.
He climbed a crooked gate
And cried, "I'll never wait.
The police will have to catch me,
I'm never going straight!"

Janeen Brian

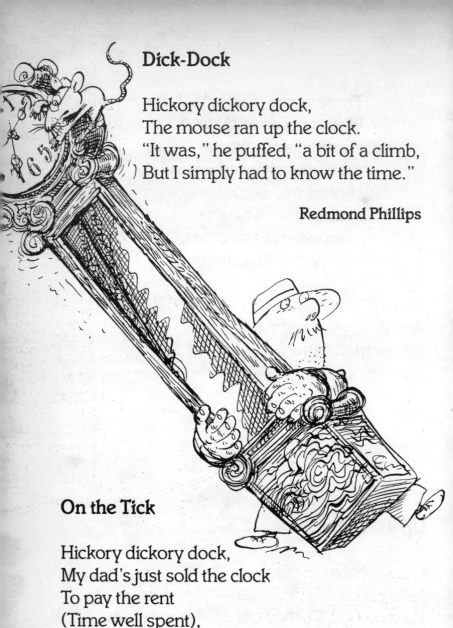

Dick-Dock

Hickory dickory dock,
The mouse ran up the clock.
"It was," he puffed, "a bit of a climb,
But I simply had to know the time."

Redmond Phillips

On the Tick

Hickory dickory dock,
My dad's just sold the clock
To pay the rent
(Time well spent),
Hickory dickory dock.

Janeen Brian

Incey Wincey Spider

Incey Wincey spider
Climbed the water spout.
Down came the rain
And washed poor Incey out.
Out came the sun
And dried up all the rain,
So Incey Wincey spider
Climbed up the spout again.

Remember this poem
Any time you might
Be tempted to think
That spiders are bright.

Michael Dugan

Up the Spout

Incey Wincey spider
Now carries an umbrella.
He won't get washed out again—
Clever little fella.

Craig Christie

Silly Billy

Little Miss Muffet
Decided to rough it—
She cooked up a stew in a billy.
Along came a spider
And sat down beside her,
So she threw him in too, which was silly.

Mary Blackwood

Who's Frightened Now?

The spider said, "It seems to me
A spider's case could worsen.
Miss Muffet has a pressure spray
Concealed about her person.

"And any spider who is lured
By pretty eyes downcast
Had better see that he's insured
Before he breathes his last.

"Her gentle charms are on display.
Do come and sit beside her?
This routine with her curds and whey
Means curtains for a spider!"

The spider shook his trembling shanks
And through his web went flitting.
"Miss Muffet's tuffet? Please, no thanks.
I think I'll miss this sitting!"

Max Fatchen

Little Polly Flinders

Little Polly Flinders
Sat among the cinders,
Warming her pretty little toes.
Her father found his daughter
Just when the sparks had caught her,
And had to put her out with a hose.

Craig Christie

Parrot Fashion

Polly put the kettle on,
Polly put the kettle on,
Polly put the kettle on.
How often must that line be said?

Polly take it off again,
Polly take it off again,
Polly take it off again—
You fill it first, you dunderhead.

Colin Thiele

Look, No Thumbs!

Jack Horner's thumb, stuck in a pie,
They may have overlooked.
I found my slice was rather nice.
I like a thumb well-cooked.

Max Fatchen

Thumbs Down

Little Jack Horner sat in the grandstand
Eating his football pie.
He put in his thumb and pulled out
   a plum
And said, "That's funny. I asked for
   tomato sauce."

Bill Scott

Jack-a-Dandy

Handy spandy, Jack-a-Dandy,
Loves plum cake and sugar candy,
Lollies, chips and liverwurst.
At eight-fifteen last night he burst.

Dan Vallely

Goodbye to Tears

Georgie Porgie, pudding and pie,
Kissed the girls and made them cry.
But their tears dried up today:
Jason Donovan rules OK.

David Bateson

Little Tommy Tucker

Little Tommy Tucker
Sings for his supper.
There'd be more to fill his spoon
If he learned to sing in tune.

Michael Dugan

Sing a Song of Sixpence

Sing a song of sixpence—
What a lot of rot!
I don't know why you're singing
As it doesn't buy a lot.

Allyson Lane

What a Peel!

"Oranges and lemons,"
Say the bells of St Clements.
But no one plays tunes
About prunes.

Max Fatchen

Thin-Skinned

Jack Sprat could eat no fat,
Until he got so thin
His wife mistook him for a twig
And tossed him in a bin.

Allyson Lane

Slick Work

Jack be nimble, Jack be quick.
Get the mop,
The cat's been sick!

Janeen Brian

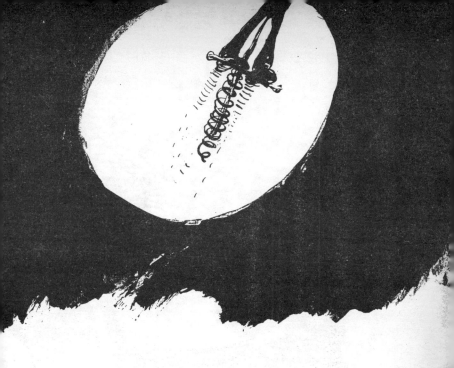

Quick Sticks

Jack be nimble, Jack be quick,
Jack tried bouncing the pogo stick.
The spring shot up at lightning pace
And shot Jack off in outer space.

Colin Thiele

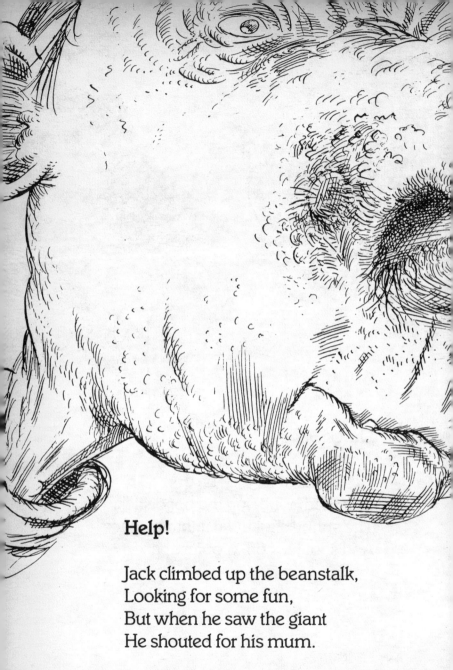

Help!

Jack climbed up the beanstalk,
Looking for some fun,
But when he saw the giant
He shouted for his mum.

Jo Chesher

Taking a Bough

Rock-a-bye, baby, the treetop may shake
For someone is guzzling and slurping . . .
That terrible wind that makes the
     bough break
Is simply my baby, who's burping.

Max Fatchen

Bouncing Baby

Rock-a-bye, baby,
On the treetop,
When the wind blows
The forester yells, "Timber!"

Dianne Bates

Just Nutting

I had a little nut tree.
It brought me nought but sorrow.
It didn't bud. It's just a dud.
I'll pull it out tomorrow!

Janeen Brian

Mary, Mary

Mary, Mary, quite contrary,
How does your garden grow?
With silver bells and cockle shells,
Because the darn snails have eaten
  all the plants!

Lilith Norman

What Rubbish!

Mary, Mary, quite contrary,
While gardening goes to sleep.
You wonder where?
She's over there
On top of the compost heap.

Max Fatchen

Quite Contrary

Mary, Mary, quite contrary,
Look over your garden wall:
With silver bells and cockle shells
You never need water at all.

Sally Farrell Odgers

Round and Round

Round and round the garden
Goes the teddy bear.
He's battery operated:
The baby left him there.

Phyllis Harry

Goosey, Goosey, Gander

Goosey, Goosey, Gander,
Why do you wander
Upstairs and downstairs
And in my lady's chamber?

It's scarcely a wonder
That she scowls like thunder
At your feathers by the door
And the messes on the floor.

Colin Thiele

A Little Bird

Once I saw a little bird
Come hop, hop, hop,
And I cried out, "Little birdie,
Will you stop, stop, stop?"

So off the little birdie flew
So high, high, high,
And he dropped a little present
In my eye, eye, eye.

Dan Vallely

Ugly Duckling

Ugly Duckling, you look cute
In your feathered bathing suit.
Your neck is long, with graceful bends;
First it rises, then descends.

Eyes alert and plumage trim,
My, you're handsome as you swim!
But as you glide along the creek
I marvel that your skin don't leak.

Wilbur G. Howcroft

Twinkle, Twinkle

Twinkle, twinkle, little cat,
How I wonder what you're at,
Up upon the roof so high,
Catching sparrows on the sly—
Never doing what you should,
Spying on the neighbourhood.

Andrew Taylor

Switched On

Please don't ding and dong your bell.
Pussy dear's not in the well.
Here she purrs with tabby belly,
Watching cat food on the telly.

Max Fatchen

Well-Wishers

Ding dong bell,
Pussy's in the well,
And four-and-twenty blackbirds
Are rather glad she fell.

Angela Sidey

A Wise Old Meal

A wise old owl lived in an oak.
The more he saw, the less he spoke,
The less he spoke, the more he heard;
Then someone ate that wise old bird.

Dan Vallely

Into the Frying Pan

Old Mother Hubbard
Went to the cupboard,
And there was a cockroach inside it.
She said, "Goodness me,
You'll do fine for my tea,"
And she took out a pan and deep fried it.

Allyson Lane

Hounded

Old Mother Hubbard
Went to the cupboard
And stared at the bone on the shelf.
She said to her hound,
"Stop hanging around,"
And sat down and ate it herself.

Max Fatchen

Cupboard Love

Old Mother Hubbard
She went to the cupboard
To get herself some mutton.
But when she got there
The cupboard was bare
Except for her husband
      . . . the glutton!

Wilbur G. Howcroft

Silver Lining

Old Mother Hubbard
Got stuck in the cupboard,
Unheard were her cries and her groans.
To end there, forgotten,
Was really quite rotten,
But at least her poor dog had
    some bones.

Phyllis Harry

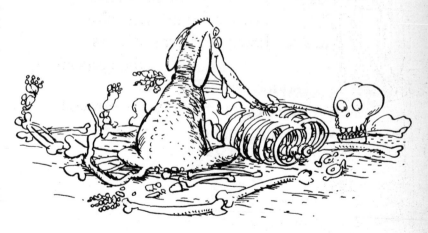

Wanted, Dead or Alive

To all squad cars, Black Forest zone,
Take care, be on your mettle.
Two maniacs are on the loose,
Big Hansel and Bad Gretel.

Last night they ate this lady's house
(To say the least it shook her),
And then they tied the old girl up
And shoved her in the cooker.

Dan Vallely

Baa, Baa, Werewolf

Baa, baa, werewolf, have you
    dined tonight?
Yes sir, yes sir, when the moon
    was bright.
For entrée I ate Billy Smith,
The main course was his dad.
His mother was the nicest sweet
That I have ever had.

Dan Vallely

Flat Out

Red Riding Hood, in quite a hurry,
Jumped into her red Ferrari,
Grabbed her bag of Granny's goods
And took the short cut through
    the woods.

The big bad wolf heard her approach
And jumped out from behind a coach.
In hospital next day, in bed,
    "What big wheels she has," he said.

Craig Christie

Pass Your Plate

"Red Riding Hood, my charming child,"
Said Grandma, full of glee,
"I have a nice surprise for you—
Wolf fritters for our tea."

Max Fatchen

Shocking!

"Little pig, little pig, let me come in!"
"No, by the hair on my chinny-
    chin-chin!"
"Then I'll huff and I'll puff and I'll blow
    your house in!"
But the wolf got a fright, and his shock
    was immense,
For the pig had installed an
    electrified fence.

Bill Scott

Catastrophic

Pussy cat, pussy cat, where have
    you been?
I've been to the laundrette to get
    myself clean.

Pussy cat, pussy cat, what
    happened, sir?
I lost half my tail, plus some hide and
    my purr.

Wilbur G. Howcroft

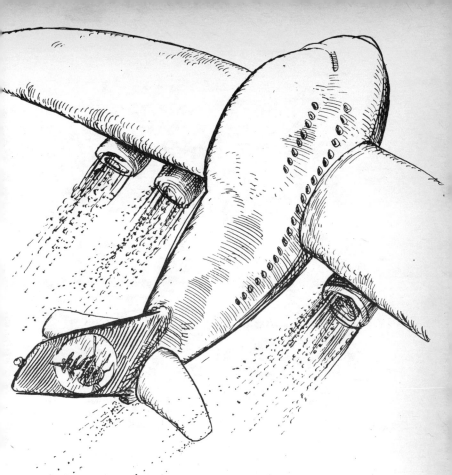

Up in the Air

Pussy cat, pussy cat, where have
   you been?
I've been to the airport at Tullamarine.
Pussy cat, pussy cat, what did
   you there?
I frightened a Jumbo jet into the air.

Mary Macdonald

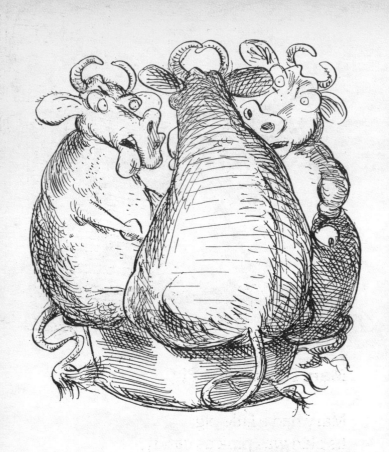

An Udder Shudder

Rub-a-dub-dub,
Three cows in a tub,
And all of them said,
"MOO-OO-VE over!"

Janeen Brian

Mary Had a Little Pig

Mary had a little pig,
Its skin was pink as candy,
And everywhere that Mary went
It followed, fat and dandy.

But when she went to school one day,
Her pig was quite forsaken.
The butcher caught it in the street
And turned it into bacon.

Andrew Taylor

Mary Had a Little Lunch

Mary had a little lamb
With gravy, mint and peas.
"Murderer!" the sheep complain,
But Mary says, "More, please!"

Sally Farrell Odgers

A Wee Problem

Mary had a little lamb
That wasn't housetrained, so . . .
Everywhere that Mary went,
The lamb was sure to go.

Bill Condon

Punk Lamb

Mary had a little lamb,
Its fleece was pink and blue.
When Mary went to the barber's shop,
That punk-haired lamb went too.
It said it wanted just a trim
And came out with a spike.
It blunted all the scissors,
So the barber's gone on strike.

Sally Farrell Odgers

Lost Cause

Little Bo-Peep
Has lost some sheep
That belong to her sister Marge.
If little Bo-Peep
Keeps losing sheep,
She shouldn't be left in charge.

Allyson Lane

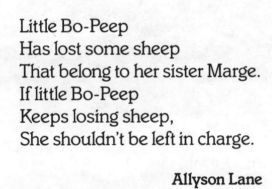

Too Baa-d

Little Bo-Peep
Can't find her sheep.
She's growing pale and thinner,
For sheep will stray;
Oh, by the way,
Who wants roast lamb for dinner?

Max Fatchen

Little No-Sleep

Little Bo-Peep
Can't get any sleep,
And there is a very good reason.
The cow's in the meadow,
The goat's in the corn,
And all of her ewes are in season!

Chris Hogan

Zzz . . .

Little Bo-Peep
Just couldn't sleep,
There was nothing on earth that would
    make her:
No potion, no pill,
No act of her will
For one second to dreamland would
    take her.
Then little Bo-Peep
Started counting lost sheep,
And now forty rock bands wouldn't
    wake her.

Phyllis Harry

Blow It!

Little Boy Blue, come blow up your horn.
The sheep's in the meadow, the cow's in
    the corn.
But where is the boy who looks after
    the mutton?
Stuck in his ear is a radio button.

Barbara Giles

Little Boy Blues

Little Boy Blue, come blow your
    mouth-organ,
The pig's in the pumpkins, the cow's in
    the sorghum.
Where is the cowboy, that indolent bloke?
Down in the woolshed, having a smoke.

Bill Scott

In the Pink

Little Boy Blue went down to the beach
With never a hat on his head.
He sat in the sun
Until, overdone—
He turned into Little Boy Red.

Max Fatchen

Wanagan

There was an old man named
    Michael Flanagan
Who went to the beach to get a tanagan,
But clouds came along and spoiled
    his planagan,
Pale-faced Michael Flanagan.

Bill Scott

The Wreck of the *Hesperus*

The boy stood on the burning deck
With badly blistered feet,
Perspiring very freely
And complaining of the heat.
Said the Captain to the Bo'sun,
"I'm a tender-hearted man.
Will you take the boy an ice-cube
And a small electric fan?"

Redmond Phillips

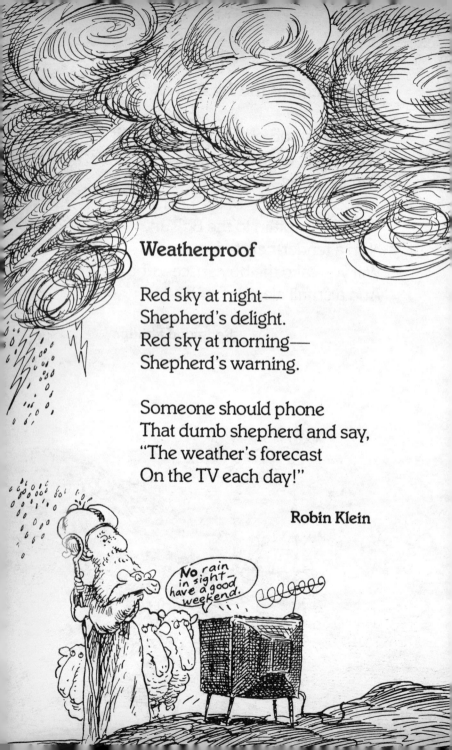

Weatherproof

Red sky at night—
Shepherd's delight.
Red sky at morning—
Shepherd's warning.

Someone should phone
That dumb shepherd and say,
"The weather's forecast
On the TV each day!"

Robin Klein

Fish Fingers

One, two, three, four, five—
Once I caught a fish alive!
Six, seven, eight, nine, ten—
Then I let it go again!
Why did I let it go?
Because it bit my finger so!
Why did I lose my cool?
Because it was a shark, you fool!

Robin Klein

Water-Mark

Robinson Crusoe
Handed his friend
A box washed up by the tide.
"It's yours, I imagine,
'Cos it's been stamped
'Use by Friday' there on the side."

Janeen Brian

Damp Dumps

Diddle, diddle, dumpling, my son John
Went to bed with his wetsuit on.
Inside's sopping and outside's dry.
There, little Johnnie boy, don't you cry.

Barbara Giles

Hat Trick

Diddle, diddle, dumpling, Elton John
Went to bed with his straw hat on.
He wore it for his breakfast,
He wore it for his tea;
I wonder if he wears it
Swimming in the sea.

David Bateson

Wee Willie Cranky

Wee Willie Winkie
Runs through the town,
Upstairs and downstairs
In his nightgown,
Yelling through the windows,
"Hey, for goodness' sake,
Turn that rotten music off,
It's keeping me awake."

Dan Vallely

No Kissing, Please

The Sleeping Beauty tossed her head
And said, "It's a mistake.
Who needs Prince Charming to arrive
When I am wide awake?
I think it's all a lot of rot.
I don't need him at all.
I much prefer, on my telephone,
An early-morning call."

Max Fatchen

Beauty and the Beast

The princess kissed the frog, which woke
Into a fairly handsome bloke
But never lost his taste for grubs
And always spoke with such a croak.

Jeff Guess

I can't—I've just washed it!

Rapunzel's Reply

The Prince: "Rapunzel, please let down
your hair.
    I need to use it for a stair."

Rapunzel: "Go away, you silly dope.
    Use some nous—and get
    a rope!"

Sally Farrell Odgers

Cold Comfort

Cinderella liked to wear
Her lovely glass shoes everywhere,
But when it came to bed, I'm told,
The prince complained her feet
   were cold.

Jeff Guess

Phew!

Cinderella drops a slipper,
And out the door she teeters.
The prince picks it up
And shouts, "Oh, yuk,
You need some odour-eaters!"

Jo Chesher

Snow White's Farewell to the Dwarves

The prince is here. I'll see you guys.
Please don't stare and criticise.
Although his socks may not smell sweet,
He's only got *one* pair of feet.

Craig Christie

Down at Heel

There was an old woman
Who lived in a shoe;
Her children were many
(At least thirty-two).
She cried with a whine,
"Oh yes, they're all mine.
But the next shoe I buy
Will be size fifty-nine!"

Janeen Brian

Footloose

There was an old woman
Who lived in a shoe.
The smell was appalling,
And so was the view,
So she packed up her things
In an old wooden box
And moved up the road
To some new football socks.

Mary Blackwood

Hark!

Hark! The Herald Angel sings:
"Ain't it lucky I got wings!"

Wilbur G. Howcroft

Dogs' Dinner

Hark, hark, the dogs do bark.
Here's something that they like—
A little treat that they can eat:
The postman on his bike.

Allyson Lane

A Dog's Chance

If all the seas were one sea,
What a great sea that would be;
If all the trees were one tree,
What a queue of dogs there'd be!

David Bateson

Index of Authors

Index of Poem Titles